I0418089

# Further Praise for
# PAGONG CANNOT CLIMB TREES

"This collection is a rallying cry, a reminder that despite the freezing nature of loss, it is by focusing one's inward gaze on remembering that we heal both ourselves and our lineages. Schwarzkopf holds all these complexities deftly, from its visceral to its meditative, all while peeling back layers of distance toward the page. Throughout we see vignettes of grief's varied states, brightened by those of love—as quilt, as foundation of house, as party, as whimsy. *Pagong Cannot Climb Trees* shows us that to live is to love."

—**CZAERRA GALICINAO UCOL**, author of *Pisces Urges*, Communications Director of Luya Poetry

"Grief is stubborn—it's traumatic and comes in waves; it stays with you and is passed down. Butch Schwarzkopf takes us on a journey spanning centuries; from the imperial violence to his ancestors and homeland, to the continuing repercussions today, and the resilience in spite of this. A deeply resonant and unfaltering collection of poems reconciling notions of home, identity, grief and growth, evoking fragments of scenes and unearthing the complexities of diasporic belonging."

—**KEZIA ARIA**, former Socio-Cultural Editor for *Vertigo* magazine and organiser for Bankstown Poetry Slam

"A revelation of the echoes of grief that fill our emptied spaces. Schwarzkopf captures the wisps of love that we try to grasp onto with heart-wrenching imagery and haunting photographs. His melodic language creates an intimacy, regardless of whether or not the reader speaks Tagalog. I smiled, yearned and saw in these reflections the diasporic grievances and rage that live within so much love. Schwarzkopf asks, where is home and how do I find my way back?"

—**LYSZ FLO**, author of *Soliloquy of an Ice Queen*

"*Pagong Cannot Climb Trees* by Butch Schwarzkopf is a collection of poetry that speaks to a generational grief, a collective trauma stark and cold. 'Inang sweeps blood… blood of her anak' is just one example of imagery that speaks to mourning and reflection and the crimson sadness associated with grief. Schwarzkopf's poetry speaks to an 'Eastern Sun' and 'cries' of long-gone ancestors that present not only the complexity of the author's background but an intriguing dichotomy between 'both colonised and coloniser'. This collection is characterized by Schwarzkopf's bold willingness to challenge colonialism and its ramifications both within and externally, whilst presenting a synthesis of reflection and mourning. This collection is daring and deserves to be read far and wide!"

—**A.R. SALANDY**, Editor-in-Chief of *Fahmidan Journal* and Fahmidan & Co. Publishing

"*Pagong Cannot Climb Trees* by Butch Schwarzkopf is a navigation of self. Reflecting on his experience with grief, he gives himself name across time and across family lineage. With care and tenderness but an unflinching honesty, trauma and family are given face, as things that 'happen to tear the fabric of reality sometimes.' This collection embodies the essence of Schwarzkopf's water sign sun: he, as pagong, riding out the waves until he reaches shore. While we may hold the hurt from the past, the lesson is not in forgetting; but rather, continuing on with hope. With language and form, this book holds a new shape for love."

—**KEANA AGUILA LABRA**, author of *Kanunay*, Editor-in-Chief of *Marías at Sampaguitas* magazine & co-founder of Sampaguita Press

"This book is an act of holding: it holds the memories of those who are gone; it holds the hearts of those of us who are left behind. Schwarzkopf is equal parts poet, storyteller, and cinematographer whose work reaches across the boundaries of geography, of time, of genre, and perhaps even across the bounds of life and death."

—**MARIA BOLAÑOS**, author of *Sana*, co-founder of Sampaguita Press

# PAGONG CANNOT CLIMB TREES

POEMS

## Butch Schwarzkopf

**Sampaguita
Press**

Copyright © 2022 by Joseph "Butch" Schwarzkopf, Jr.

Pagong Cannot Climb Trees
Published by Sampaguita Press
Sampaguita Press LLC
P.O. Box 731305
San Jose, CA 95173

www.SampaguitaPress.com

All rights reserved.

For information about permission to reproduce selections from this book, please contact SampaguitaPress@gmail.com.

Cover and book design by Sampaguita Press
Cover artwork by Carlos Manalo
Author headshot by Killian Pham and Noel Bare, firstandlasts.co

ISBN 979-8-9857712-4-4 (paperback)
ISBN 979-8-9857712-5-1 (ebook)

This publication is made possible by funding provided in part by the Yerba Buena Center for the Arts and other generous contributions from our readers. We offer our heartfelt thanks for your support.

For Manuel Jose and Leticia Schwarzkopf

## Note to the Reader

This book is about grief.

These poems focus on the grief of losing loved ones, a homeland, and self. The grief of erasure, imperialism, and the abuse (physical, sexual, emotional) enacted by our colonisers. The grief of child abuse and intergenerational trauma.

This is a chapbook about grief, with a hope that somewhere I/we/someone can find healing.

As you read on, please be mindful of your own grief, that some of these words and content may trigger yours. Please take care of yourself and your mind.

# PAGONG CANNOT CLIMB TREES

# CONTENTS

## Pour One Out

Things happen to tear
the fabric of reality,
sometimes.

# LIBING

# From the end of time:

I swipe down to refresh but there are no new posts
posting gave out long ago
just like the Internet gave out long ago
and electricity gave out long ago
and water gave out long ago
and breath gave out long ago
I heave in slowly, my chest expands, but no air enters
the atmosphere around is flat, there is space but nothing within it
not even miniscule particles bouncing around
almost like the eerie stillness you feel on a windless morning,
when the only sounds you can hear
are your own shoes on the gravel
and a dog barking in the distance
but the gravel here makes no sound
and there haven't been dogs in these parts in a while just
unenviable quiet
and if there was still blood pumping in these ears, perhaps we'd hear
    that but
there is no sound but the unending beeping of a faulty Google Home
    device, getting mystery notifications from the past, unable to
    restart
but you can't really hear it, just feel it, like haptic feedback in your
    fingertips, but softer, gentler, and unceasing
and so I sit at the end of time
waiting for the end to the end
throwing stones into the ether hoping one will drop down on me and
    save me from this miserable non-existence, bato bato sa langit,
    but gravity gave out long ago, so the stones just float away
like our memories
half recalled voices, faces

fuzzy

as if trying to make them out through gauze, but

the mind isn't so clear now, it is full of gauze and not much else

just shapes of figures, like that ghost I once saw as a kid in Kalibo,

    an outline of a being once lived, an outline of a life once been

a life that should've been experienced but was spent living and

    breathing

but regret gave out long ago

and there is nothing left to do now but throw stones and sit and stare

    at this empty screen and refresh.

# Manuel

Before your breath

I dreamed you and saw you and thought you
and knew you

and lost my breath

coughing, spluttering, led through grey
corridors to see you and meet you

and you, short breaths
and breathing

and clasped hands and closed eyes and small

alive

and held breath

and sighed relief as you fell asleep, and rocking,
and rocking, and rocking, and rocking

and warm breaths

as I held you and told you and taught you

and heavy breaths

as you lay there sleeping and we watching and
waiting and willing and wishing and wanting
and dreaming

and breathless

as you lay there smiling and watching and
waiting and willing and reading and knowing
and teaching

us

Then exhale –

and no breath –
and cold, the smell of clay
and rigid and clasped hands and closed eyes
and small –
and then kneeling and crying and begging
led away through black suits to black car to
black streets to blank

heart.

After your breath

I dreamed you and saw you and held you
and knew you.

# ASWANG

After *Aswang* by Alyx Ayn Arumpac

Inang sweeps dugo, not yet honey-thick, into the kanal
her walis, stained, frayed, flicking droplets across the kalye
across her tsinelas, across her exposed toes
across her dreams like every panalangin unanswered
every sentence unended, every life unfinished
o kaya finished too soon. Those final hininga
fading before the sunrise, failing like prayers for mercy
to the smiling aswang, snuffed out, swept away,
yung dugo sa kanyang walis, dugo ng kanyang anak, natokhang.

## Minsan:

nakita ko kayo
o baka, narinig ko kayo
o kaya, naalala ko kayo


on the wind, sa hangin
bigla kong naramdaman yung warmth niyo
that could fill a room like the smell of bawang cooking
yung radiance niyo
as if, nakatabi lang tayo doon sa kuwarto niyo habang naglalaro kayo
    ng solitaire


but I'm on my balcony and you're not here
kasi matagal na tayong nag-goodbye


noong araw na binisita niyo ang panaginip ko
nakaakbay kayo ni Lolo
walking up the driveway of Raby towards that old white van
at lahat kami nandoon to see you off
umiiyak kami pero tumatawa lang kayo
kasi after so many years you were together again
and you told us it was going to be okay


and it has been, pero it hasn't been
kasi okay naman ako pero namimiss ko po kayo
kasi okay naman kami pero it's not the same without you
our family is uncentred without you
and I am ungrounded without you

because it's been 7 years since I last put your hand to my forehead
it's been 7 years since I last hugged you
it's been 7 years and I've grown up
and I have so much to share with you:

Lola, gumraduate na ako, marunong na ako magdrive, naging
    teacher ako, na-publish ang mga poems ko, gumawa ako ng
    pelikula,
nagpakasal na kami ni Tiffany.

at alam ko na magiging proud kayo sa akin, kasi po,
masaya na ako.

# Sunlight

I think of you at dawn,
when those first rays of purple light
flood my bedroom window
with that 1940s haze of a time gone by, like
waiting
for the right moment to speak, but letting
all the other voices drown you out –
Brother, I'm cursing time for
burying you
in the earth, and leaving me
on it – you could've used it
better than I have –
as this hue fades,
giving way to Eastern Sun
it's the warmth of you
that lends me the strength
to –

# LIVING

# Bahay

You come home
kumakanta sila, palaging kumakanta
wumawagayway ang sintonadong boses nila sa bahay
dancing with the aroma ng adobo, kumukulo doon sa kusina

yung mga Tita mo, your aunties, nagtsitsismis habang nanonood sila
    ng teleserye
they're making fun of 'you know who' and praising your latest
    haircut
all in the same sentence

yung mga Kuya at Tito at kapit-bahay mo, all the men, nakaupo sila
    sa kalye, gathered around a tiny lamesa
alas quatro palang, at lasing na sila
nagbibiro at tumatawa, the same jokes they laughed at kahapon at
    nakaraang lingo

yung mga bata, tumatakbu-takbo sa bahay, sumisigaw
as they duck into the kusina to steal another lumpia or two

yung Lola mo naman, nakaupo sa pinakamabuting posisyon para
    makita ang lahat, over seeing all and smiling to herself, nakangiti
    sa sarili nya
masaya parin, kahit magulo

and you, swatting langaw and stepping around every silya at lamesa
 habang bumabati ka sa bawat isang elder
touch the back of their hand to your forehead
'Mano po, mano po'
then you greet your mother with a kiss and your sister with a hug
and you steal a silya, pagkain, and join in the kaligayahan.

# The fabric of existence

I am the good morning towel my mother trapped between my sando and my back,
       comforting Chinese cape of my childhood, a thin shredding material
I am my sister's baro't saya, worn as a primary school cultural day costume,
       home sewn from dollar store tartan scraps,
       simulacra of our culture
I am the filipiñana my Lola treasured for special occasions,
       matching brooches, and earrings, and rings,
       the classic Filipina glow up for friends and feast days
I am the custom barong tagalog I wore on my wedding day,
       all piña-jusi off-white half opaque thoughts
       and intricately patterned words
I am the alampay my wife didn't buy in Manila,
       delicately detailed, soft, sheer and structured,
       but when will I wear this in Sydney?
          When can I be Filipino in Australia?

# CTRL+Z

_____ meanders through the mind, steady,

silent…

inconsistent

touch, like horned Ronin burning through synapses

tattooing anxiety to the walls of your psyche

and rightly you fear what you might…

~~be~~ ~~do~~ ~~see~~ remember.

# Balat

I hate the colour of my skin
    the colour I can't bear to wear
    the light bright white
        with undertones of pink pigment –
reflecting my ancestry
reflecting 400 years of occupation,
for I am both colonised and coloniser.

You see, deep within I know who I am:
cut my skin and I bleed my culture
my ancestors dwell within my lungs, blessing each breath with their history
my tongue cries the knowledge of my people
my hands bear the marks of their legacy
but then I look in the mirror,

And I remember I am the result of the invader,
the men who took my people from their hills and their rivers
            from their boats and their villages
forced them to work on farms
forced them to dress European
forced them to toil all day, reap our land for their riches, and then pay them
    the taxes.

You see, we were born warriors
but we were raised enslaved
first they invaded our lands
        our bodies
          then our minds

took our history

our names

and our voices

purged our Gods then taught us to bow to their White GOD

taught us to pray to their White GOD

taught us to beg that their White GOD

would deliver us from *their* tyranny

then they took our children and put the poison of their Devil in them

they spread their seed without discretion

held our people down, forced themselves upon us as a lesson

why do you think they called it 'missionary position'?

It was their job to rape. To bring us Civilisation.


That's what I am


a civilised product of their unholy blend

their attempts to mend our culture

and bend our will to their demands

my lightness is the stain of their sins.


I will never wash their guilt from my being

for it hints at a history more mestizo than Filipino

more konyo than indio

and as much as I may untrain their lies from my mind

I hate the colour of my skin.

# Dugo

A woman is born under Spanish subjugation, trains her tongue in
    coarse Spanish inflections
and bears a son through American violence, and her son grows up
    to battle Japanese invasion,
and his youngest anak is raised under a ruthless dictatorship and
    flees and has
You, torn from your homeland.


The sumpa of oppression lingers in your bloodstream, a parasite
eating
and eating
away at your thoughts
generation
upon generation
infecting your words
your voice
your heartbeat
your being
with the violence of kolonyalismo, the same colonialism that
tells our daughters, hijas, to bleach their balat, cover their bodies,
    subdue their speech,
tells our sons that they are animals rabid with desire, just waiting to
    be unleashed
tells our government that any criticism is terrorism,
tells our police that they can murder the poor with the mere whisper
    of shabu,
tells our leaders to erase and displace our Indigenous Peoples,
    to plunder and invade ourselves

every day renews the covenant of the blood compact

a mixture of the dugo of our kababayan and the colonisers' lason,

    and You

You drink from this chalice too

with every sip that further condemns our homeland, You

lapping at the droplets that spill from the cup

finding western words more comfortable on your tongue

spewing the toxicity that says to sit down instead of rise up

        to pray instead of act up

        to be grateful, thankful, joyous for what we have

        don't question what we don't

licking morsels of false salvation til you forget

who you are

who your father was

who his father was

who his mother was

who her ancestors were

til all you can give your children are shadows of who we were

and a cup empty

of what we could've been.

# My Nose is Always Blocked

I've never known that stench of heavenly blood that soaks the earth after a
    shower,
but I feel that wafting honey sweet stickiness that comes with it.

I've never known why the scraping hum of a car passing by
                (you know, that sound of rubber on asphalt, of cylinders
                pumping, of fuel igniting)
                                fills me with dread,
but I love the bitterness of waving goodbye.

I've never known how the bite of the cold on my skin on a crisp winter
    morning recharges my mind,
but I know how little it takes to drain me out again.

I've never known why there are days where I can't see the point of it all
                (you know, those days when you can't find your keys, and
                you panic because you can't find your keys, and you know
                you left them somewhere around here, but if you can't find
                them then there's really no point in going out, so you stay
                in bed instead and think about that time your grandmother
                died?),
but I know that one day I'll feel better.

I've never known a great many things,
but I know that I'm willing to learn them.

# My people

My people are not of dust
but sea and wind and bamboo,
We fell to the puti's lust
but will rise as the tides do.

# Supermarket

After Allen Ginsberg

I wander through Woolworths seeking the spirit of Walt Whitman

My wife hunts for fettucini in aisle thirteen

The trolley is new, it has a cup holder. I miss the way the old ones would swerve to one side, so that walking in a straight line was more like trying to coax a stubborn mule

I quote Ginsberg as I reach for the Coco-Pops and choose Froot Loops instead

She doesn't understand sequential numbering

She's currently in aisle one

Something about expired milk

I drift between stands, nearly taking out a rampaging child, what a shame

Aisle three

The staff eye me as I rummage through Red Rock Deli chip packets, trying to pick the freshest bag. It's always the one with the most air

Aisle ten, flour

I throw a pack of $3 Old El Paso tortillas into the pile, pondering if Kerouac enjoyed soft shelled tacos

Now she's in eight after Kraft boxed cheese

An old man is talking to the mops

*Hey man, do you need any help?*

He shivers, eyes glazed over

*Mind your own business!*

I haul-ass out of the way and continue idling, waiting…

She's still trying to find cheese. It's in aisle seven.

The lights are uncomfortably white

*What time is it?*

*No idea…*

a blight in the time-space continuum

a state of perpetual liminality

I keep on walking and ask myself, *would Burroughs prefer Nutella or Vegemite?*

# ACT II, SCENE VIII

INT: BEDROOM - NIGHT

CHILD sits at a black desk

in a castle of books

filled with descriptions of how to make fried ice
cream, how to code pop song ringtones 222 5 77 8
33 long press * 6, how melanin makes eye colour

filled with little poems, songs, sketches, wishes
in the margins, between lines, behind covers

Child sinks back into the uncomfortable plastic
chair

stomach bruises from step-father's fists aches

Child falls asleep.

CUT TO:

INT: SHOWER - DAY

ADULT awakens on the floor

of the shower, in a pool of lukewarm water

the water keeps running

how long has it been running?

Adult's shorts are soaked, stained with a black
sludge

mouth tastes of corn chip mush, and something
else, bitter, throat burny

mouth tastes of repressed memory, or rather
ignored memory

Adult stands and turns off the water

stomach churns from half-digested alcohol

Adult falls out.

                                        CUT TO:


INT: HALLWAY - AFTERNOON

POET walks to the slim standing mirror

stares at own eyes, brown, with flecks of green,
not in the pretty way - in the marble you don't
want so you trade it for a sandwich way

how much melanin accumulated to form this colour?

smells their shirt

smells of popcorn, and spilt vanilla coke
no sugar, and something else, bitter, throat
scratchy

wonders have they been here before

Poet looks into mirror and sees Child reflected
back


                    POET:

                does it get better?


                    CHILD:

                it has to


stomach says a quiet prayer then breaks apart,
shards of skin filling the room, strings of guts
fall to the floor, blood rushes forth and crashes
against glass

poet falls to the floor in a heap of bones and
intestines

poet falls.

# RE-LI(B/V)ING

# Diasporic sigh
## or: Pagong cannot climb trees

Homebound to a place that was never your home:
the place of your blood
but not your body,
the place where the air fills the shape of your lungs
but not the place of your first breath
and probably not the place of your last.

Homebound to a place that was never your home:
the place of your ancestor's ashes
where the last inklings of their spirits settled in the soil
   in the water
   in the trees,
the place of your first thoughts
where your voice first made sense
but not the place of your first words.

Homebound to a place that was never your home:
a home that was never your place
the place that shaped you through the hands your Lola
stirring kare kare into the base elements of your soul,
the place that tastes like home but doesn't look like it
the place that feels like home but doesn't smell like it
the place that drew the outline of your being but didn't colour it in
the place where you sprouted, but not where you were planted
the place of your kapwa, your anitos, and your kaluluwa.

Homebound to a place that was never your home,
  but will only ever be home.

# B*Y*N*

After Keana Aguila Labra

My mother tells me of half recalled grandparents
With possibility of tainted blood, of self destruction
Of women who hid with their sisters from the lust of invaders
Of men with mestizo features and possibility

She doesn't want to age
My mother tells me of half recalled grandparents
Ones she barely met and ones she carried with her
With possibility of tainted blood, of self destruction

Of women who hid with their sisters from the lust of invaders
Shaking between unsolid structures, clutching hands
Of men with mestizo features and possibility
Wasted for the white man's salvation

We do not, we can not speak in other stories
We only reminisce on the faint shadows of ancestors.

# Staccato

After Jose Garcia Villa and Miles Davis

In, a, silent, way,

Lighter, brighter, echoes, dance, on, heavier, tones,

Groans, quietly, humming, under, sea,

Ever, constant, quivering, rumbling, reverberating,

Veins, dripping, melted, honey,

Trumpet, sanding, over, Morning's, eye,

Fleet, footed, Piano, brushes, fingers, through, the, lashes,

Bass, holding, breath,

Waking, Morning's, slumber.

# ANITO

The Ancestors whisper legacy in the smog-laden fissures of your brain
encode messages through firing synapses - an ancient inception;
which thoughts are yours, and which were written down the unending lines
   of succession?
which words are yours, and which were blown into the shape of your
   mouth, echoing through the cavity of your awakedness?

they stay with you,
reside in your hands and feet
age/time-less drivers of your life-full shell
taking action when your heart hesitates,
not your inner voice but your impulsive twitch:
the one that makes you step into a room, but forget why you came there,
the one that tells you of the family names that you were never taught,
the one that dreams with you, to say goodbye in their final moments, before
   you even know that they've dissipated -

The Ancestors tell you secrets in the placement of stones, the passing of
   lizards, the direction of wind
they ache in your bones til the day that you join them, and still
they lay the path for your footsteps, brush away the leaves before footfall,
   and soften the blows.

They remember you as you were before your existence, they recall you as
   you exist.

# Greetings

I had never really known you 'til I met you –

    not the outside shell you but the hidden behind a thousand layers you,

        the unsolvable puzzle wrapped in barbed

        wire you,

      the need to know basis you.

The you that I met on the day that I realised I was going to marry you as I
    crumbled behind a car on the

corner of the street uncontrollably weeping, mourning my grandmother and
    you held me

and in those arms I met a love that I couldn't even begin to reciprocate

and so I vowed in that moment to spend the rest of my days aiming to
    match it.

I just hadn't told you yet.


And now I have.

And now we're walking down this aisle

hand in hand –

This is it,

what I dreamed of when I was six

when my world fell apart and the separation of my family left a hole in my
    heart

that nothing could fill

    and I prayed that one day that I'd meet you.


But I'm still meeting you

because how much can one person ever truly know another?

I'm every day learning a new facet of you,

I wanna spend every day learning a new facet of you,

I'm gonna spend the rest of my life every day learning a new facet of you.

I'm gonna learn the tongue of your ancestors,

    gonna learn to say "gwapa kaayo ka,"

        learn to say "nahigugma ko nimo."

I'm gonna parade with you through the streets of Cebu holding a figure of

    the baby Jesus above our

heads, dancing to the rhythm of your culture.

I'm gonna swim in the waves of your roots in Boljoon.

I'm gonna learn who you will be by loving who you have been.

I'm gonna spend every day relearning you so that in 10, 20, 30, 40, 50 years

    I'm still going to be getting to

know you.

And every day I'ma re-meet you. So I may as well start here, with:


Hi my name is Butch, it's nice to finally meet you.

# NOVENA

Response (All): Have mercy on the soul of _____
Leader:         An altar
        lined with photographs printed at Officeworks
        surrounded by holy icons
        candles burning slowly
        scattered arrangements of flowers
            Mourning,

Response (All): Have mercy on the soul of _____
Leader:         We gather,
        fill the loungeroom with echoed chanting
        read off tattered papers passed on from one family to the
        next
        in endless repetitions ingrained in familial lines of tradition,

Response (All): Have mercy on the soul of _____
Leader:         Day after day after day
        'til the tears dry up and the wailing stops
        and the laughter starts and we remember the moments that
        brought us to-

Response (All): Have mercy on the soul of _____
Leader:         And even if you don't believe it
        you still do it because your parents told you to
        and their parents told them to
            and their parents told them to
            and their parents told them to

following down the voices of the ancestors

'til you reach the first Filipino whose beliefs were erased and

replaced with Christianity

because it brings you a sense of peace even you don't

understand,


Response (All):  Have mercy on the soul of _____
Leader:          All those who've passed away
                 and all those who will pass away
                 and as you grow older you repeat these prayers over and
                 over 'til you don't need the paper anymore and you pass it
                 to someone younger because you know all the words already
                 and every time you say them you see the faces of your lost
                 ones
                 and you know, in your end, they'll say these prayers for


Response (All):  Have mercy on the soul of _____
Leader:          You.
                 And they'll gather 'round an altar, framed with photos of
                 you
                 surrounded by holy icons
                 candles burning
                 voices chanting
                 tears falling for you.


All:             And may perpetual light shine upon you
Leader:          May you rest in peace
All:             AMEN.

# Notes
# & Acknowledgements

# Publisher's Note

The Tagalog and Cebuano phrases found throughout the collection are translated into English in the following Translation Index.

We translate these phrases into English for inclusivity purposes in respect to our non-Tagalog and non-Cebuano speaking readers, particularly BIPOC and non-Tagalog and non-Cebuano Filipinxao readers. We also translate these phrases in order to adhere to the requirements set by some book distributors.

We are aware of the compromise we make in order to make this art more accessible to a wider audience. In translating these phrases, we participate in a global market that continues to be dictated by Western- and English-supremacist practices. We are also aware that these simple, direct translations of words fall short in communicating their cultural weight and meaning.

We acknowledge the history of translating devices used violently as tools of white gaze revisionism, for the cultural erasure and othering of non-Western, Global South, and diaspora art. This includes the related practice in the United States publishing industry of italicizing words from non-English languages. Our current policy is not to italicize these words.

As cultural discourse, translation methods, and language resources evolve with the times, so may our formatting and translating practices at Sampaguita Press. It is our dream and goal to be able to have our titles commercially available and translated into different languages other than English, for greater language and literary equity.

# Translation Index

**Titles**

  Pagong - turtle or tortoise

  Libing - burial/funeral

**From the end of time:**

  Bato bato sa langit - "Throwing stones at the heavens"; the
  first half of a Filipino idiom, "Bato bato sa langit, ang
  tamaan wag magalit" ("Throwing stones at the heavens,
  whomever is hit shouldn't get angry")

  Kalibo - Capital city of Aklan province, on the island of
  Panay, Philippines.

**Aswang**

  Aswang - evil mythological beings, e.g. vampires

  Inang - mother

  Dugo - blood

  Kanal - gutter

  Walis - broom

  Kalye - street

  Tsinelas - slippers

  Panalangin - prayer

  O kaya - or (else/rather)

  Hininga - breaths

  Yung dugo sa kanyang walis - the blood on her broom

  Dugo ng kanyang anak - the blood of her child

  Natokhang - killed, extrajudicially, by police or military, in
  relation to Duterte's war on drugs

**Minsan:**

  For full poem translation, see page 59

**Bahay**

  For full poem translation, see page 61

**The fabric of existence**

  Sando - singlet

  Baro't saya (baro at saya) - blouse and skirt, a traditional
  Filipino dress combo

  Filipiñana - a traditional Filipino formal dress

Lola - grandmother
Barong Tagalog - a traditional Filipino formal shirt
Piña - pineapple fiber
Jusi - banana leaf fiber, sometimes more recently silk/ synthetic silk
Alampay - traditional Filipino shawl, usually lace

## Balat

Balat - skin
Mestizo - a Spanish colonial term for Mixed (native and foreign)
Konyo - rich, Spanish/English speaking families
Indio - a Spanish colonial term for Indigenous people

## Dugo

Dugo - blood
Anak - child
Sumpa - curse
Kolonyalismo - colonialism
Hijas - daughter, younger girl
Balat - skin
Shabu - crystal meth
Kababayan - countrymen
Lason - poison

## My people

Puti - white

## Diasporic sigh or: Pagong cannot climb trees

Pagong - turtle or tortoise
Lola - grandmother
Kare kare - peanut sauce stew
Kapwa - self in other(s)
Anitos - ancestor spirits
Kaluluwa - soul

## Anito

Anito - ancestor spirit

## Greetings

Gwapa kaayo ka (Cebuano) - you are so beautiful
Nahigugma ko nimo (Cebuano) - I love you
Boljoon - a municipality in Cebu, Philippines

# Full Poem Translations

## Minsan: (Sometimes)

I see you
or maybe, I hear you
or perhaps, I remember you

on the wind, on the wind
I suddenly feel your warmth
that could fill a room like the smell of garlic cooking
your radiance
as if, we were just sitting beside each other in your bedroom while
  you played solitaire

but I'm on my balcony and you're not here
because it's been some time since we said our goodbyes

on that day when you visited my dreams
you, holding hands with Grandfather
walking up the driveway of Raby towards that old white van
and we were all there to see you off
you laughing, as we cried
because after so many years you were together again
and you told us it was going to be okay

and it has been, but it hasn't been
because I'm okay but I miss you
because we're okay but it's not the same without you

our family is uncentred without you
and I am ungrounded without you
because it's been 7 years since I last put your hand to my forehead
it's been 7 years since I last hugged you
it's been 7 years and I've grown up
and I have so much to share with you:

Grandmother, I graduated, I can drive now, I became a teacher, my
     poems got published, I made a film
Tiffany and I married

And I know that you are proud of me, because,
I am finally happy.

## Bahay (Home)

You come home
to singing, always singing
their joyous, toneless voices wafting through the house
dancing with the aroma of adobo boiling away in the kitchen.

your aunties gossiping while watching a soap opera
making fun of 'you know who' and praising your latest haircut
all in the same sentence.

Your brothers, cousins, uncles, and neighbours, all the men, sit in
    the street, gathered around a tiny table
4pm and already drunk
laughing and joking, the same jokes they laughed at yesterday and
    last week

the kids run through the house, yelling
as they duck into the kitchen to steal another spring roll or two

whilst your grandmother sits at the greatest vantage point,
overseeing all and smiling to herself, smiling to herself
it's joyful, even if chaotic

and you, swatting flies and stepping around every chair and table
    greeting every single elder
touch the back of their hand to your forehead
'(Your hand in) blessing please, blessing please'
And you greet your mother with a kiss and your sister with a hug
And you steal a seat, a bite, and join in the merriment.

# Author's Notes

**Manuel** - First published as a video poem on YouTube: https://www.youtube.com/watch?v=99f5eMz4Uf0

**Aswang** - Written in response to the film *Aswang* by Alyx Ayn Arumpac

**Bahay** - First performed at Multilingual Poetry Slam 2018

**Balat** - Parts of this poem were integrated into '500 Native Tongues,' a group slam poem written in collaboration with Andrew Cox, Tanvir Islam, and May Tran

**My People** - Written in a tanaga poetic form

**Supermarket** - Inspired by "A Supermarket in California" by Allen Ginsberg

**ACT II, SCENE VIII** - Written during The Digital Sala poetry grind and inspired by the poets of The Digital Sala

**B\*Y\*N\*** - Previously published in *Marías at Sampaguitas* Issue 2, July 2021 ("Mahal, Who We Are, What It Cost Us, and How We Love"); and *Marías at Sampaguitas* website, November 2020: https://mariasatsampaguitas.wixsite.com/marias/post/poetry-by-joseph-schwarzkopf-jr-butchoy
Written in the Labra form developed by Keana Aguila Labra

**Staccato** - Written in the comma poetry form of Jose Garcia Villa and inspired by "In A Silent Way" by Miles Davis

**Greetings** - First performed as part of my groom's speech during my wedding reception

**Novena** - Inspired by and taking lines from the "Novena for one who has died" as documented by Our Lady of Guadalupe Church

### Interior Photography

All interior images photographed by Butch Schwarzkopf
Holga 120FN, Ilford HP5 400 Plus 120 film
Yunon YN500, Ilford SFX 200 35mm film

### Translations

Credits to Christian Aldana S. for assistance with many of the translations provided at the end of this book.

# Acknowledgements

Thank you:

To my wife Tiffany, loml, my day one, the biggest supporter of all my random endeavours - you inspire me to keep going.

To my family, the Schwarzkopf clan, always the loudest people in the room, I owe my voice to you all. Shout out to my dad, The Pogs, in particular for always showing up. To the Sitjar-Roma clans, thank you for accepting me into your family and your unconditional support.

To my friends, thank you for your constant encouragement, the laughs, the adventures, the late night Cabra runs, the philosophical questions - you are all in this work.

To my poetry friends and mentors, The Digital Sala folks, the Luya Poetry team, Bukid Baddies, and all the other virtual friends I found during the pandemic (there are too many of you to name individually but you know who you are), you helped me write again after I'd given up on poetry.

To my editors, Asela, Keana, Maria, and Nashira, thank you for making sense of the jumble of words I came to you with. To the rest of the Sampaguita Press and Marías at Sampaguitas team, this work would not have been possible without your care and consideration.

To my beta readers, Demitra Olague, Christine Andrada, Francesca Lingan, and Iris Orpi, thank you for your advice and for seeing the things I couldn't. To my blurb writers, Kezia Aria, Lysz Flo, Czaerra Galicinao Ucol, Lorenz Mazon Dumuk, A.R. Salandy, and Keana Aguila Labra, thank you for your time and kind words. To my cover artist, Carlos Manalo, thank you for so beautifully capturing the vision for this chapbook.

Finally, to you, person reading this, thank you for sharing in this journey of healing with me.

# About the Author

**Joseph "Butch" Schwarzkopf Jr.** (he/him) is an Illawarra (Dharawal Country) based Filipinx poet and filmmaker. His works deal with diasporic culture, colonialism, and generational trauma. He has performed as a poet at events such as Outspoken Poetics, Unspoken Words festival, and The Digital Sala's Tula for Typhoon Relief, and competed in the Bankstown Poetry Slam Grand Slam, and APS Multilingual Poetry Slam. His works have been published in the *UTS Writers' Anthology*, *UNSWeetened Literary Journal*, *Australian Poetry Anthology*, *Mascara* literary journal, and *Marías at Sampaguitas* literary magazine. *Pagong Cannot Climb Trees* (Sampaguita Press, 2022) is his debut chapbook. His short film, "Body," was a finalist in Made in the West, Sydney Lift-Off, and Cebu International Film Festivals. His biggest claim to fame is appearing in the background of *Shang-Chi and the Legend of the Ten Rings* for 0.5 seconds. He can often be found wandering the aisles of his local Kmart, driving to Cabramatta for late night bánh mì, or practicing Filipino Martial Arts in his backyard. His favorite word is pie.

## About the Artist

**Carlos Manalo** is a queer Asian American Pacific Islander, originally from the island of Saipan in the Northern Mariana Islands. He currently works in Portland Oregon as a graphic designer and illustrator. In his free time, Carlos enjoys watching cartoon shows while feasting upon Hot Cheetos.

# Land Acknowledgement

The majority of this book was written on Dharawal Country, with some pieces written in the traditional lands of the Gadigal people of the Eora nation. Sovereignty has never been ceded. It always was and always will be, Aboriginal land. This book was also produced on the unceded lands of the Ohlone People.

The staff at Sampaguita Press acknowledge we are settlers on the stolen sacred lands of these Peoples. We remember their connection to these regions and give thanks for the opportunity to live, teach, and learn in their traditional homelands. May we create connections with them, and may we learn Indigenous protocols to become honorable stewards of the land.

We encourage you, Reader, to:

• Amplify the voices of Indigenous people leading grassroots change movements
• Donate your time and money to Indigenous-led organizations
• Politically support the Land Back Movement

In line with these encouragements, Sampaguita Press supports Indigenous art and donates a portion of Press funds raised to Indigenous-led organizations.

In reflecting on our own lives and remembering our family histories, we must remember the legacies of colonialism that we have benefitted from and continue to benefit from as settler-colonialists.

From Palestine to the Philippines, none of us are free until all of us are free.

# About Sampaguita Press

Sampaguita Press is an independent micropress publishing house based in San Jose, California. We publish works by and for artists of color. We acknowledge the intersections of identity and support the LGBTQIA+ folk/x in communities of color as well.

Sampaguita Press was founded in 2021 by poets and creatives who wanted to create a space and platform for ourselves, our peers, and other fellow voices who are underrepresented in mainstream publishing.

We strive to inspire progressive change. We acknowledge that change is made with solidarity. We honor and nurture the relationships between our fellow communities. We especially seek works that broaden perspectives and foster understanding.

We believe in racial and social equity. We acknowledge that Western literature and publishing are still overwhelmingly white spaces, and we are committed to amplifying underrepresented voices by providing attention and care to artists who may not have access to traditional publishing spaces.

We are an intersectionally feminist & womanist, inclusive press. We prioritize artists of color of all genders. We discourage hegemonic narratives; hierarchical structures; and supremacist, assimilationist, and normative messaging.

We are a safe literary & linguistic space, and we welcome chapbook submissions in non-English languages.

We support Indigenous rights and sovereignty over the land known as the United States. Our support goes out to the Indigenous groups everywhere in the world who have been harmed, silenced, and displaced. We encourage our readers to learn about and support Indigenous Peoples.

Look for the next title from
**Sampaguita Press**

# The Water We Swim In
## by Christian Aldana

Christian Aldana's debut poetry chapbook, *The Water We Swim In,* is an ode to radical care. Through community organizing and deeply held love, Aldana follows in the footsteps of Grace Lee Boggs against a carceral state. They champion safety for all who need it while challenging the waters of our time, this state in which protection is needed. Aldana questions the broken system and shows us an alternative future well within our grasp. As she gives to others, she also gives to herself, allowing space for grief, acknowledging the distances between us in the diaspora. Unapologetically queer and neurodivergent, Aldana's writing exudes power and teaches us we will never drown as long as we have each other. Empowering, mobilizing, and unrelenting, *The Water We Swim In* is a poetic revolution, a manifesto for all who believe in fighting for more.

Visit www.SampaguitaPress.com to learn more.

www.ingramcontent.com/pod-product-compliance
Lightning Source LLC
Chambersburg PA
CBHW060255150626
46553CB00019BA/2333